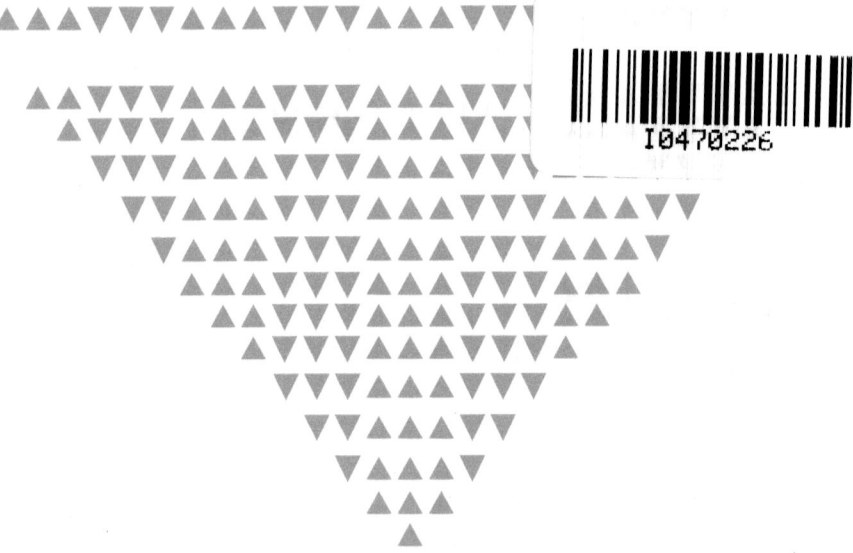

Copyright © January 1, 2017 Morgan Drolet and Shawn Sullivan

All rights taken.

ISBN-13: 97809985205-13
BISAC: Art / Annuals

Volume Four in *Annals of Los Angeles*

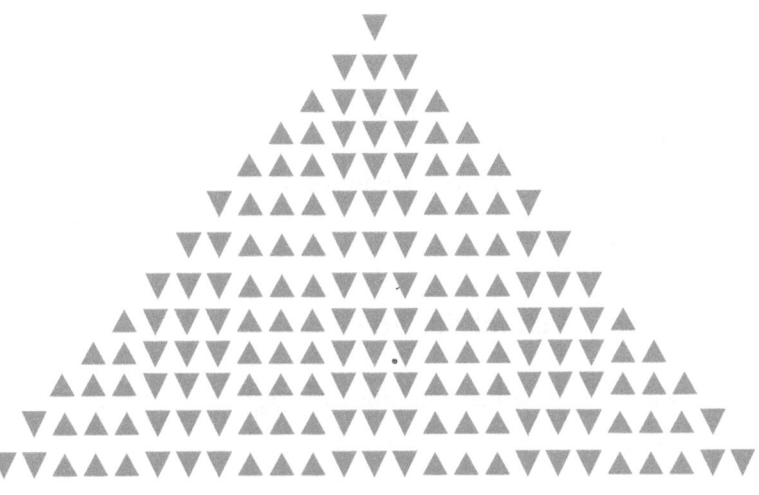

# NEON BURRITO PUBLISHING

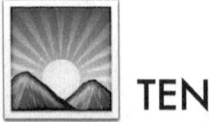 TEN

IRL: Los Angeles, California

URL: Neonburrito.info

☞ Dedicated to Patty Smyth

"Isn't it funny, I should be laughing"

☞ Morgan Christopher Drolet

This could be a simulation? Hats off to the programmer.

☞ Shawn Michael Sullivan

An unlicensed practitioner of regular and fabulous mistakes.

# BAK ER'S DOZ EN

# 1,

You wanna hear some bullshit?
It's a choice to be happy.
See, I told you.
Bullshit
Let me back pedal
It is a choice, but like,
one you have to keep making,
every second of every minute of every day
until you're too senile or too dead to make any more choices.
And in all those seconds of minutes of days of years,
you have to be aware that there is a choice to be made
And then,
Struggle of all struggles,
you have to make the harder choice-
To be happy.
An uncritical, accepting, joyous state (happy)
        you may say
is the natural spirit of human emotion
One that has been convoluted,
corrupted over time.
But I wonder—
        If fruits hard won are the sweetest,
shouldn't happiness by virtue of its very nature be a struggle?
So you can choose to be happy.
It's just the hardest of choices
and requires hyper-vigilance indefinitely.

Or maybe it's as simple as
it sounds.

If you have the answer please mail to:
1847 1/2 Gramercy
Los Angeles, California

## 2,

He was so tuff
The toughest. That's why
he'd bought the cobra head belt buckle

He took out his woman
Knowing he was tough. That
cobra head belt buckle would explain
He knew she loved it
because it made him look tough and
she liked dating tough guys
that was another part of why he'd bought it

At the bar, black light catching the bone the fangs
He liked how smooth it looked, that cobra head belt buckle

It wasn't
why he'd bought it

but it was a bonus

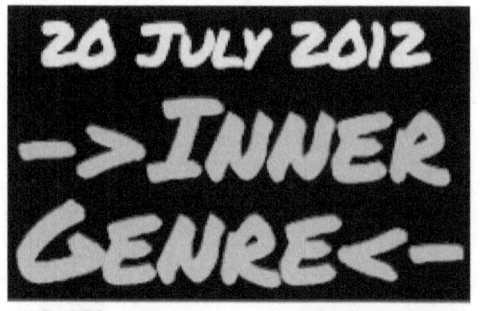

# Chilly Scenes of Winter

**Yesterday Is Tomorrow a.k.a. A Past Letter to A Future Self**

LABELS: 70S, CHILLY SCENES OF WINTER, JOAN MICKLIN SILVER, QUOTE, ROMANCE, ROMANTIC

"Susan. Susan always appears to be happy and normal. She must know something."

CHILLY SCENES OF WINTER
a fizzling romantic drama from 1979
directed by Joan Micklin Silver

Suspect I would've preferred the 1976 novel *Chilly Scenes of Winter* by Ann Beattie to this 1979 movie directed by Joan Micklin Silver. This story of a man who becomes frantically and neurotically obsessed with a woman suffers from a kind of gloomy, sticky intensity; the result of neurotic excretions and a tendency to emphasize, tonally and thematically, the neuroses. Realworld neurotics orbit their fears around dramatically rich specifics that appeal to creative types as enhanceable details.

The match-up is corny, tedious, obvious. The method is common to movie narratives because movies tend to limit their tonal palettes, while novels tend to have more textures and perspectives. Not all movies do this and not all novels do that, but in my opinion the first step toward making a boring anything is limiting your tonal palette. I believe a narrative should be like knocked over beer dripping from the edge of a table. I can think of at least a handful of neurotic, obsessive, male-centered romance movies from the 70s and 80s, and they're all damaged by a sweaty-palm nervousness.

So we're all on the same page, this is my personal definition of neurosis:

neurosis |n(y)oŏ'rōsis|
noun ( pl. -ses |-,sēz| )

mental incapacity to be mellow, for more than
like two seconds

Charles (John Heard) romances co-worker Laura (Mary Beth Hurt), his affection for her as immediate as his attraction. She's six weeks into a marriage separation.

"If I make you feel terrific will you marry me?"

Charles swiftly angles for Laura to move in with him, which she does. He adores her. She's everything he wants. She's unsure. While living together, Charles begins to worry there's a problem with the relationship and he hounds Laura with needy insecure questions, creating problems through his worry.

The love Charles has isn't the same kind of love Laura seems to be looking for, or rather, Laura isn't sure what she's looking for and wants space to decide, but Charles crowds her because he's so sure.

The relationship lasted two months and occurred before the movie's narrative.

Laura returned to her husband.

The relationship is told through flashbacks, and the narrative takes place a year after the break up, when Charles begins to act on his longing for Laura.

He breaks a long radio silence, by calling Laura and asking to see her. Before the call, he promises himself not to beg.

She agrees to see him.

Seeing her makes him desperate to have her again.

"Why would you choose someone who loves you too little over someone who loves you too much?"

The movie excels when it handles character emotions with tender earnestness. One can sense the flames of desire between Charles and Laura, and sense his fevered passion, and her earnest confusion. My fav thing about the narrative is how it renders a compassionate portrait of romantic despair.

The melodramatically suicidal mother of Charles is probs my fav character.

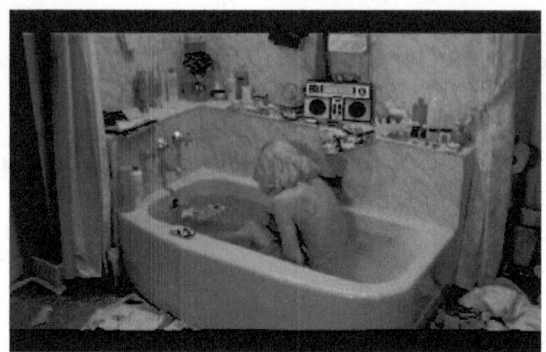

"I think one day she just decided to go nuts because it's easier that way. That way she can lie around in the bathtub, and say whatever she wants, and hit the scotch whenever she feels like it, and just not do anything. Sort of tempting, isn't it?"

I like the mother's excessive mania which, though it instigates drama, doesn't seem to seek or mean to create drama. Charles is an emotional tornado, his mother is the storm in the sky.

## Q: How do you feel?
## A: Slow jam infinity.

cars on Fairfax make some noises

all right, okay

for fun i holler *hi how are you*

miscellaneous shit is my lifestyle

cosmic energy, part of eternity

no one sees me, believes me, worries me
tonight

**3,**

We went to the arboretum
the arboritarium, she called it
We tried to find a pneumonic device and settled on:
    What are you going to do with those sandwiches?
        I'm gonna arboretum
She said— now I've got it

**4,**

Above the kitchen sink
The open window
Air feeling like just down wind from a bonfire
This is November I guess
An air compressor vocal outside in a rolling boil
This apple dented in several places
Most noticeable at the spot I dropped it on the ceramic floor
       The tile is fine

I think: I am blessed
I think it over and over for a minute trying to believe
while
I chew an apple (dented)
I think, after that minute: I think I believed I am blessed-
at least half the times I thought it
The other half of the times I wasn't paying the strictest
attention to what I was thinking
Plastic trash can wheels roll outside and
the rumbling sounds huge
Bigger than I know the cans to be

It's hot and my nose is dry to bleeding so
every few hours I jam a glob of coconut oil up each nostril
Coconut oil, white before melting to clear inside my nose
I sniffle some of it up and back through
my sinuses down
my throat
down
Coconut oil tastes like coconut
Olive oil tastes not like olives
I don't know what castor tastes like

**5,**

Each time the 720 passes through skid row, me on it trying to believe

that some people
some mornings
wake up in those tents and It feels like a good morning

camping

## Always dying, sometimes laughing

[immediate overshare:
nothing reasonable delights me]

i don't understand dark humor, really
really it's not understandable, it's my favorite

a room full of people sometimes
might mention to me with silence
and/or inform me with sideways glances
that my form of dark humor isn't funny
certainly not admirable, actually not interesting

but only usually does reality give me that feeling
and that's just reality's opinion

during those moments i mention something else
for example i might bring up *Melmoth the Wanderer*
why the hell did i bring up *Melmoth the Wanderer*

i sort of treasure blundering moments, or rather
i'm used to being who i'll always be
me
i've got my pros and cons

## Begun on a Valvoline postcard I was using to bookmark *The Moviegoer*

staring at everything
horrible and
staring again

yup, more life

bearing the unbearable
strength through the unbearable
helps me realize
oh, that hadn't been unbearable
my bad
who cares (whoever witnessed)

manic or hilarious
this world is one of them at anytime... sometimes both
they can feel the same but they're not
nah

## 6,

She sat there with him. Absently
holding onto something gray.
Watching, but not so closely as to
make him uncomfortable, to not seem observing
There are three or four plastic containers of food
lids piled to the side in an upside down pyramid
It is cool there
In the shade of their alcove. Cool enough that
his blankets remain at his shoulders and around his feet
So far he hasn't spoken a word but
This isn't so unusual
A bus passes. Glinting points of sun reflect its orange
skin to catch his eye in the shade
In the shade where the light has not yet reached him today
Stopping chewing the rice
Plastic white spoon hanging on air
above the largest container and, eyes only, following the rolling star
He will be finished soon
It looks like today they won't speak
But tomorrow she'll bring his favorite meatballs. Maybe that'll coax him
out

## Everything's Fine, Thanks

then why do i go outside?
i don't know, because the outside calls me
why it calls me i don't know

could it be Ohio...
is that my childhood in the country i hear?

like i said, i don't know

## 7,

What's up
How you been
Oh I know him
He got a brother, a twin
I know him from middle school
His brother got a baby
Your brother got a baby now
Right?
On the way
Yeah and I got a baby too
That's where I'm goin right now
Ta see my baby and my girl
Whatchu been up to?
We goin to work
I'm tryin to get me my own place
Again?
After I meet up wit my girl and baby Ima be lookin for a job today
          No shit?
You should come work with us
Whatchy'all do?
Telemarketing
Right up here off Western
And I kin come in today?
Yeah they probably hire you today
Ok, shit, cool
Ima go meet up my girl and get the baby and stop by
Not off Western it's Mariposa actually
They just fired someone so they'll probably hire you today

The bus eases up on western
The three debark
The young couple turning left toward telemarketing
          The young man right, toward a woman and a baby

## It's the Clock that's Moody

time passes me without glancing back

during my good days, mediocre days, bad days
all my days, everyday and whatnot

time passes me without glancing back

i don't care just kidding i worry
time left never returns

when all my time has left me forever
i won't be the one who knows what then

# Weird... Or?
# Oh I Get It (Pretending)

what's so, so, soooo weird
or weird enough or whatever
is
i'm like
yeah
through the day and such
some days
i'm like
*today is bad*
often, i think
i can be like
*oh today is bad*
in my room
you know
trapped in my bad
there i go through the bad
in my room
alone
so bad
yeah

then i go outside and see the sun and i'm like
oh
*oh*
yeah well
*okay*

**8,**

I often make assumptions about a person in an instant
by their appearance or
posture
so if I'm passing You on the bus
(You're on a corner) it's
safe to say I'm
thinking about You
picturing Your life based on all the things I know
all the things I've seen
but maybe that moment
You in it
isn't the most of the time You
what if Your just high or
self conscious
have forgotten how to stand
but then, if those are You're problems
We have that in common at least

## Hombre, That's a Technicality

because, then:
oh... i started talking about CVS, but you said CBS...

you said CBS, i heard CVS
why does anything happen ever
i mean seriously

and the other day:
a couple months ago when Morgan visited
i brought out a George V. Higgins book to quote from
i opened *The Friends of Eddie Coyle* and immediately
i said "cosmic" because immediately
i found underlined the quote i wanted to read

"I'm a very cautious man," Jackie Brown said. "I plan to sit here for about two
        hours and maybe I'll nap a little. In the meantime, every car..."

i read in a totally appropriate tone
until i began to tone down
then i began to stop reading upon realizing
        heheh
that wasn't the quote i'd wanted to read
i noticed quite a few lines in the book were underlined
        nothing cosmic had happened
then i did some page turning and eye scanning
until i found and read the intended portion

            "This life's hard, but it's harder if you're stupid."

[i'd started at the adorable beginning of course

        "I'm afraid of horses. I like the moonlight."]

side story:
i remember working an overnight and telling a coworker
*i want to work smart, you know, definitely*
then i did some dumb shit

which had been expected anyway
fuck

the ongoing story:
recently my cousin posted a John Wayne meme
above the following quote there was a photo of John Wayne

"Life's hard but harder if you're stupid"

horseshit, i thought
and sure enough Snopes totally agreed, John Wayne never said that

familiar with this quote i mentioned its true source
(mentioning facts is considered an annoying characteristic of people
who are called hipsters)

my cousin didn't reply to me after i mentioned the quote's true source
my cousin had vibed the quote, hadn't pondered its truth
he's an Ohioan, his feelings are his truth
he also once shared a meme of Abe Lincoln saying

"I hate Michigan"

my cousin voted for Trump
i'm a person who made myself up in a Los Angeles apartment
we're family

**9,**

The sky was full of crashing waves
Frozen in motion
Leaking heavy
A plane dips avoiding
their reach
A dark mountain of velvet
hangs down from above or

A black puppy makes chase
leash dragging through
parking lot Chinese laundry

## Day-Glo Radioactive Overrated

true, true, sure sure, thanks for bringing this up
indeed during life moments i might think —
          *later i'll be writing*

as long as i have my tomorrows
i'll have my reasons to write
          — my life's logic

my personal bullshit
<u>as</u> <u>if</u> life is words — <u>as</u> <u>if</u> i'd rather write than live
<u>as</u> <u>if</u> reality fits and belongs on a page
one can't live to write, since life exists outside a page
that's an absolute fact and why nonfiction is nonsense

also — that thing not worth writing about, that thing i won't
               name now nor mention again
see it then forget it, that unnamed thing is also part of why
the concept of nonfiction is utter malarkey

it's all fiction once it's words on a page
[and the past is reality sealed in a tomb]

the life value of writing:
i forget, no wait i've never known

i've heard loneliness is the lowest life category
what is the life value of reading
i wonder while wondering if anyone reading is ever alone
and i'm not mentioning something else i'm wondering
plus, now i realize that while reading one can still be lonely
i remember *The Heart Is A Lonely Hunter*

[lingering overshare:
          i used to say i want to write of life
          that was and is true but also i'm
          a phantom in my reality]

## 10,

I remember watching my grandparents die for years
It seems like they were in and out of hospitals
slowly turning to chalk
   Blue veiny thin chalk
for the better part of my childhood
I remember taking my grandma's extra wheelchair
hands struggling to keep up with the wheels
as I flew down the hill behind their house
Trying to skid around the corner at the end

## 11,

I am so scared and sad
and
angry
and
depressed,
so consumed with worry, so much of the time.
I wonder if everyone could feel this way.
As if I'm giving myself away 24/7, but
never in the ways I want to,
the ways I hope for,
or
in any of the ways that will
make a difference
Keep dreaming, someone might suggest.
oh I will
but,
sometimes there's a lotta time ina day

# Holy Shit

we're at the table and i mention
i'd like to be eaten

i'd like to be in a relationship
with a cannibalistic woman
who could eat me if she wanted to

then the table becomes quiet
oh

is anyone thinking about me thinking about
the body as a temple

then i mention
(this is another day with other people)
i mention that thanksgiving should be cancelled
and halloween should be made a federal holiday
(seems obvious to me)
"not sure i'm with you on this, shawn"
i hear

basically
anytime
i
imagine
i'm
being
dangerous

# Symbolosm

no this problem wasn't noticed beforehand
that's how this became *the problem*

yeah, sure —
once noticed, a problem can be fixed if it can be

but i find everything most interesting at the start
this which became *the problem* by not being noticed
now noticed why must it change from what it is (pushy)

the nature of a problem is to be a problem and
all problems are perfect examples of themselves

from an artistic perspective they're relatable
symbols of imperfection within all human existence
individuals often first notice this during their teenage years
often referring to this as the human condition when they grow older

what does an artistic perspective insist?
everything is as is

some people look at problems & notice only problems
which is lame
and it's okay to be lame, sure
since it's okay to have problems
okay

the worst that happens is risk
and i'm dangerous sometimes, depending

though i know for sure that no problem within existence
is more important than existence

## 12,

The black asphalt mimics the bubbling surface of
a coy pond at feeding time
The rain sounds of crumpling wax paper
Cars skate by on stilts of white gold
Streetlights through the drops perched on my glasses explode
shimmering stars of green yellow red
The falling tears are larger beneath this foliage
but less frequent
They wrinkle these pages with wet waves
The ink smears a watercolor form
Blue words looking like escaping
Someone materializes from a brick wall, swaddled in cotton
hurriedly relieving a bucket of outside water gotten in
then tucking back to brick
Cars sweat rivulets sucking in light
The older ones belching heat and smoke or steam at intervals
Electric signs project melting marshmallow reflections on the pavement
Wind whistles changing direction and
the rain finds a way to attack from the side
The branches seem as disoriented as me
I can see the burning letters
nestled in the sky at One Wilshire
See the cranes that reach through the night
I picture myself stranded atop that wet metal ladder
Having only to climb down but paralyzed
My Vans squeak as I shift my weight
I am falling
Another squeak and the bus sneezes up to the curb
Windows replaced by foggy opaque heat in slipping streams
Winter in Los Angeles can be hard to pin down
but checks in now and then
Must be we haven't had enough traffic lately

## 13,

I am on the corner of Fairfax and Olympic when I hear it
The flat thud so hollow
it doesn't even echo
The sound of a nearly full plastic bottle hitting the floor as I turn
through the blue-dark morning
  I am in front of the Pioneer Chicken stand
I see the car and the body
The car sliding gently
Back right tire coming to rest upon the curb
Too far still to tell if the body is resting or...
Moving toward it I am telling the 911 operator
Olympic and Genesse
He asks me to repeat
Asks my phone number
Two men stand over a body
writhing
Looking concerned
The one with the round face
and mustache
a phone to his left ear
The woman from the car approaching in pink
  Dark in the dark under the lights
  of slowly passing cars
scrubs
Blood on the face of the woman on the ground
She wears scrubs of a mint green
They are both moaning
but in different ways
The woman from the car seems frantic
I feel frantic
I stand looking at the bloody face
The pool of blood with its spittle trail
leading from somewhere

I tell her help is coming
Moan
I tell her
"Everything is going to be OK"
"Shhhhhhh"
"You're going to be fine"
I wonder if she is dying
As her eyelids spring open I
watch the pupils roll down from their checking on her brain
Focusing
  Or trying
to focus on me
"Shhhhhhhhyou're going to be OK"
I wonder if she is paralyzed
A small group has gathered
and a man up the street is attempting to divert traffic
His best air traffic controllers tai chi
Traffic pays him no mind
The sun moves like the woman's eyes over the horizon
"Don't move" I say
Repeating what the paramedic had told me on the phone
Two men are jogging toward us
West on Olympic
Their scrubs match the bleeding woman's
She nods her head and wiggles her legs
to show them she can
The pool of blood has not gotten larger
I head east lighting a cigarette
Momentarily forgetting
my coffee has gotten cold

a screenplay with the tentative title *Eye of the Storm**, co-written by Shawn, Kendrick and Richard

saying
"that's like life"
while being exposed to art
is funny
because
everything is life anyway
all of life is all of everything
everything is actually life
life is bad art is life
i'm bad art, actually

overwondering:
have i heard enough positive quotes to conquer today

just fundering how many positive quotes i've heard
how much gas i have in my engine

obviously my car is still running, here i am am going
positive quotes behind me
positive quotes ahead of me

hell yeah, cool
was just fundering
which is my style
i don't get it
peace

**Richard doesn't like the title**

# dissimilar to anything else ever based on this title

*plop plop* — my sneakers — *plop plop*
across Oakwood sidewalks toward La Brea

what are the houses around me like? sometimes i look at them,
sometimes windows allow me affectless visions of interiors, mostly i
don't think about them

lots of them have these curved rooftop tiles which are orange and
something international and the residents are mostly traditional(?)
Jewish people who seem nice when i pass them on sidewalks

today while walking i'm figuring out what i've figured out
that a person who thinks life is a fight tends to be
thinking what i'm thinking

sharing sympathies — no thanks
*if we share let us share the fight!*

others who feel caught in an endless battle called life
always my kind of people
i search not for those who will fight against me (common)
but for those who will fight with me (rare)

# NEON BURRITO PUBLISHING

DIY since 2016

the feels since birth

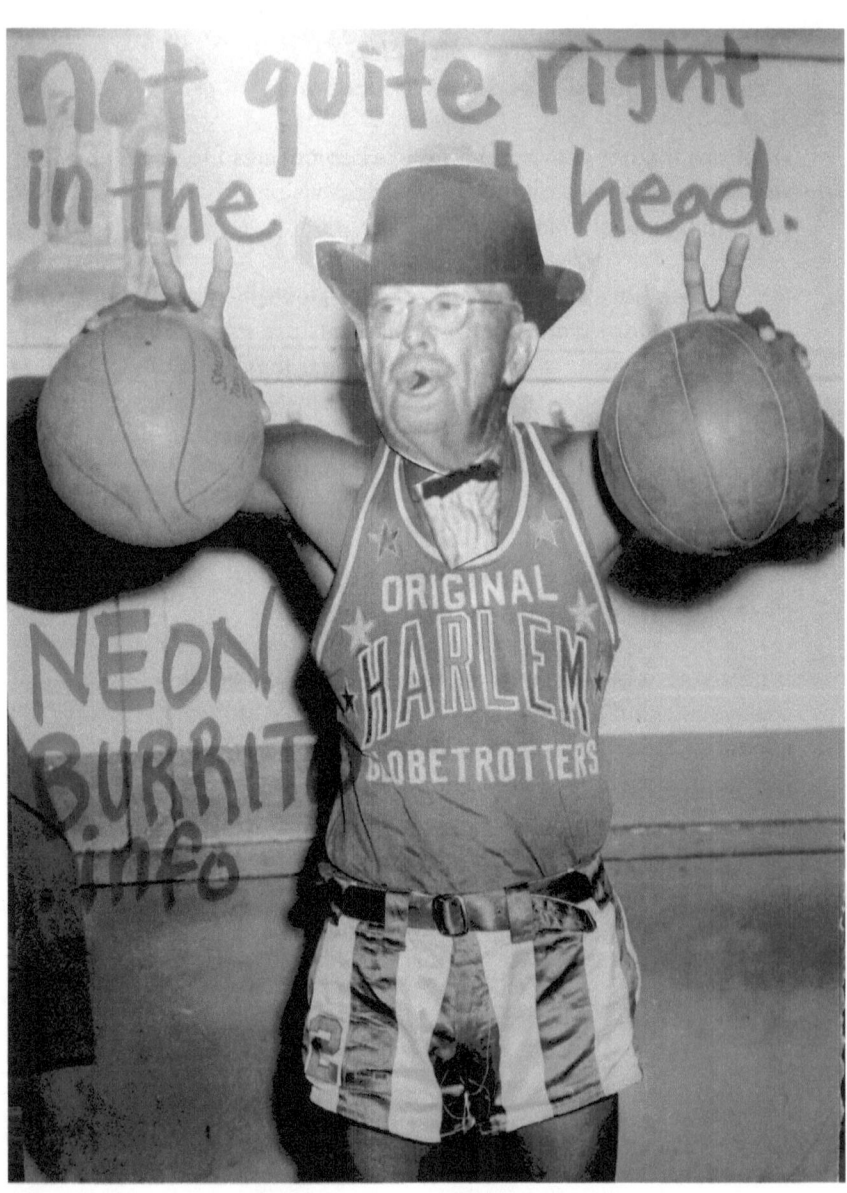

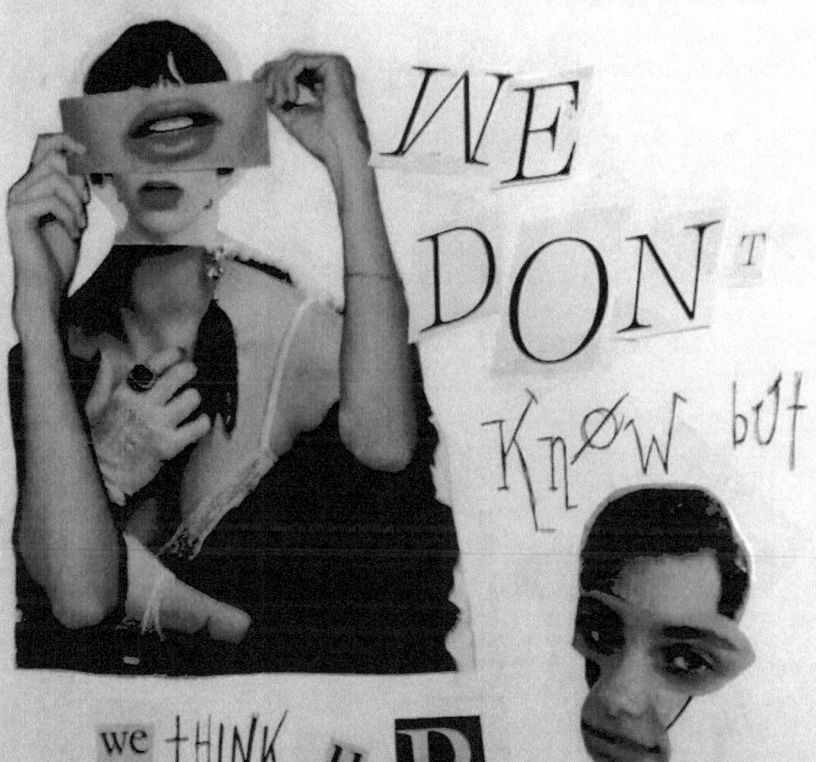

## Poetry Without Poems

we getting along is rare

paradigm shifting is everything

because a man can see inside his own eyes at least a little

is when i know some bullshit is happening

i don't keep remembering as much as i keep reading

unretatable except by virtue of similar idiosyncratic unrelatability

the well-known days of heaven
when do those last forever
i'll wait impatiently for the answer okay

and this is what I do:
here's a good reason the world feels like this to me

here i go: first of all i'll say something else i imagine in my future

then i start doing dumb shit to pass time and i can't believe it

i relish small endeavors and nap between them

not in the mood to be down

problems from last week don't matter today

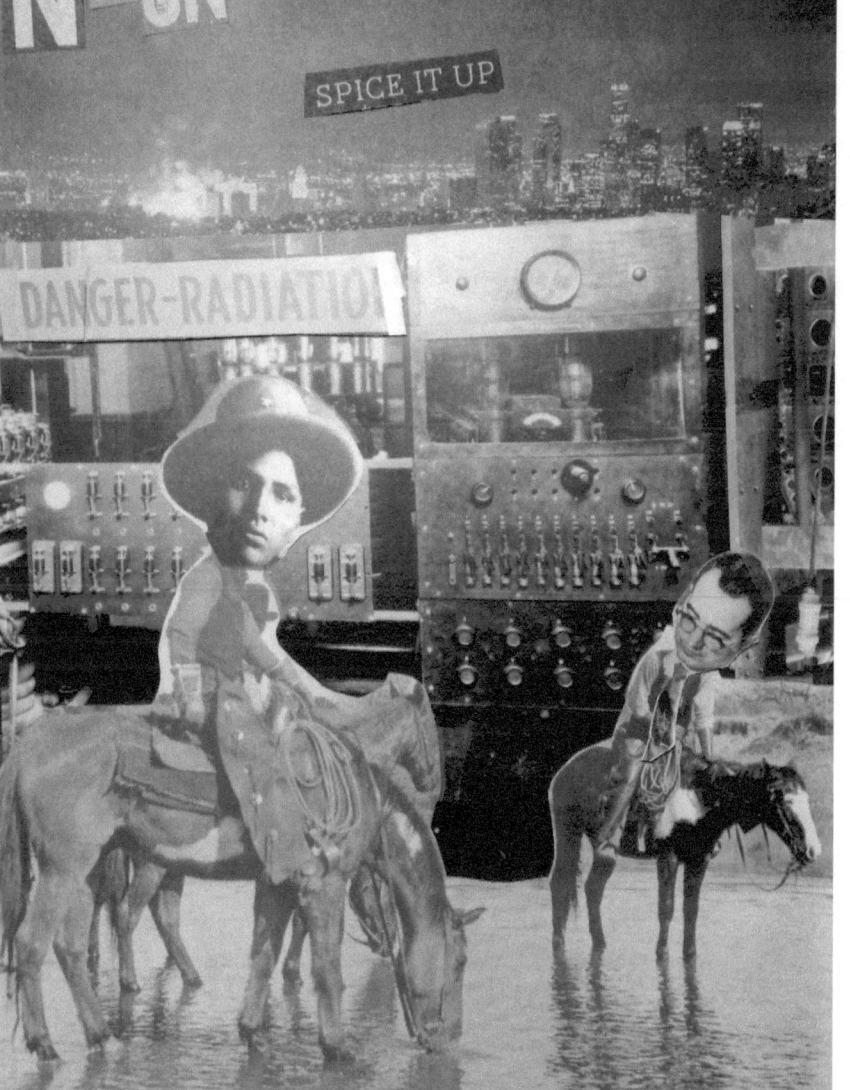

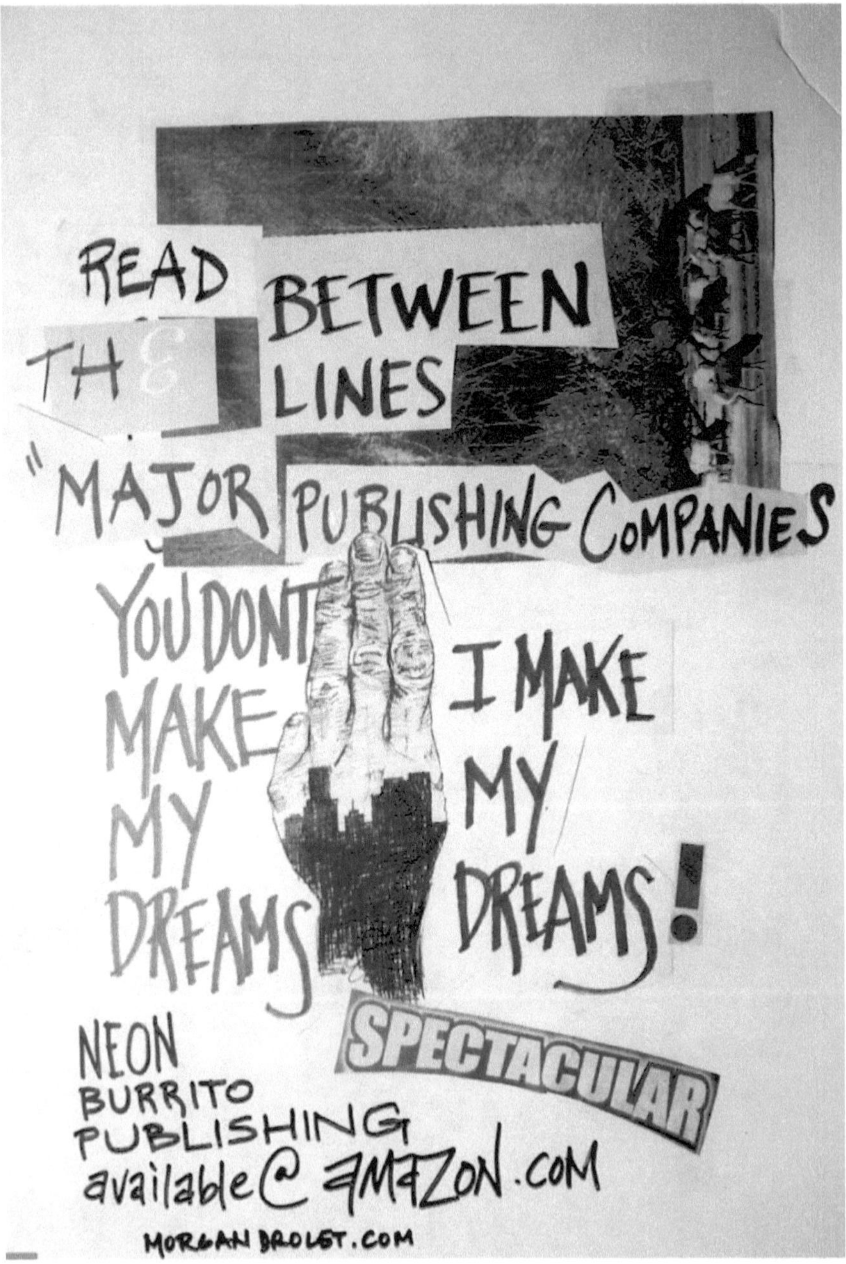
READ BETWEEN THE LINES
"MAJOR PUBLISHING COMPANIES
YOU DONT MAKE MY DREAMS
I MAKE MY DREAMS!
SPECTACULAR
NEON BURRITO PUBLISHING
available@ AMAZON.COM

## Single Lines

All the beautiful things continue

Everything is just sometimes

That was a way of mourning my life while I lived it. I want to be done with that now

He directed his glance at me. I felt injured. But I wasn't

When I see you there, I think about how we are a head's turn from being in each other's lives

You'll never get a clearer view of society than the bathroom of a gas station/IHOP

I want to bang a shovel over the horizon

Days of living off change

He smoked cigarettes like there was an answer at the bottom of each one.

Ferociously stoned

Some of the funniest things I've heard, were whispered by ceramic figurines

Opossum terrorizing the front of a liquor store

She had a hairless cat named Rapunzel

A raw stench like a riverboat full of cattle

Life as a death sentence

Smoke Five and the Highland Park Opera House usher were in love

Standoffish porpoise

This, a rigid gulp from tarnished tin

A desaturated psychedelic thief does a solitary bumpngrind in a calm blue coat

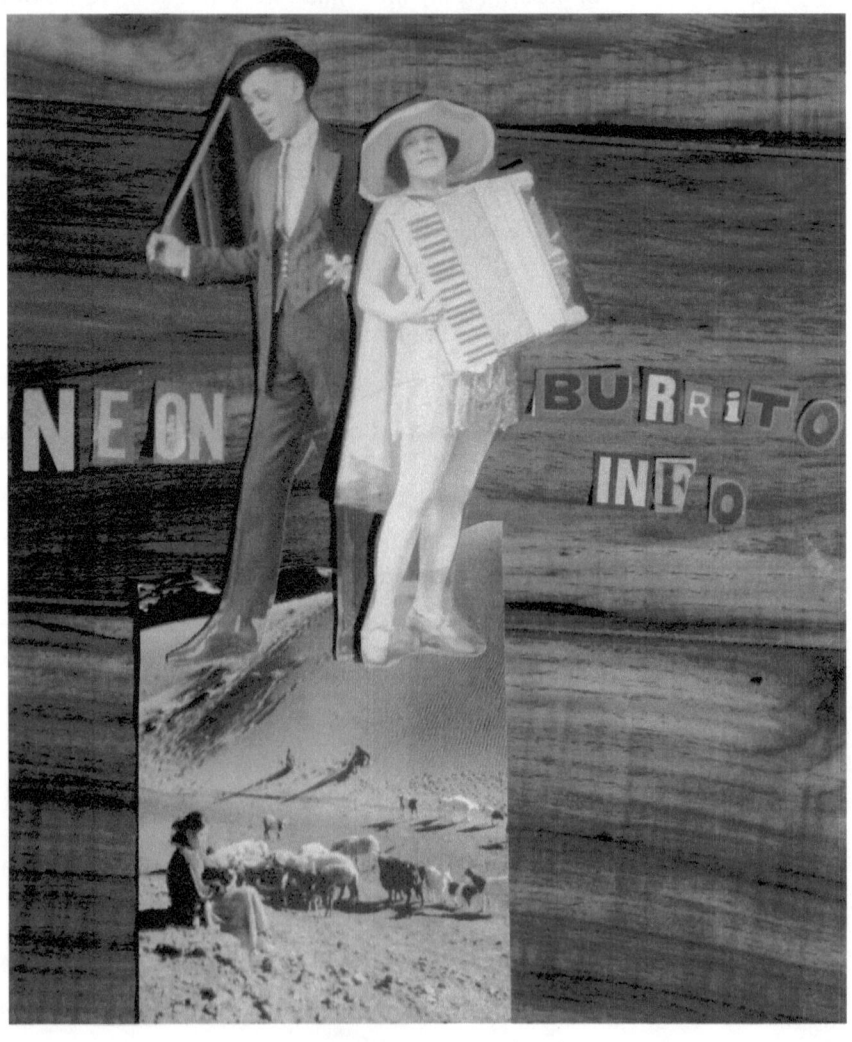

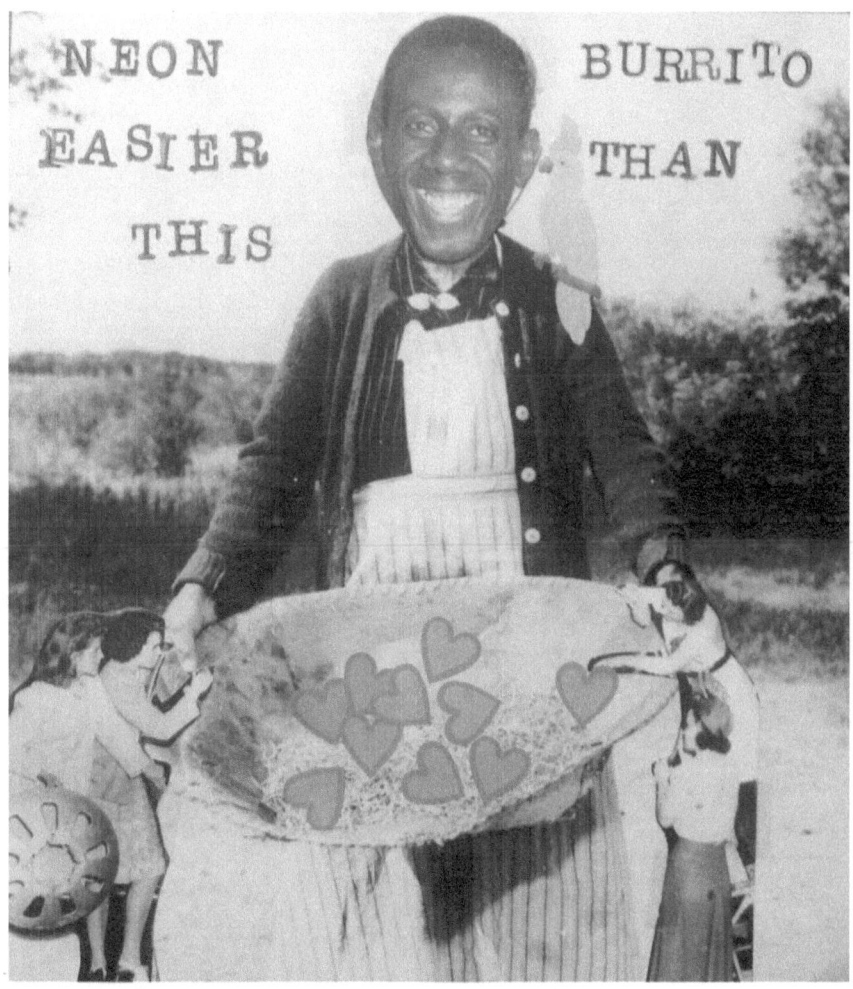